The Lighthouse

Patrick Vitullo

www.auctuspublishers.com

Copyright© 2022 Patrick Vitullo

Illustrations, Book Design, and Cover Design
by Colleen J. Cummings

Published by Auctus Publishers
606 Merion Avenue, First Floor
Havertown, PA 19083
Printed in the United States of America

All rights reserved. Scanning, uploading, and distribution of this book via the internet or via any other means without permission in writing from its publisher, Auctus Publishers, is illegal and punishable by law. Please purchase only authorized electronic edition.

ISBN 978-1-7368278-5-7

Library of Congress Control Number: 2022942154

Foreward

Patrick Vitullo's poems become more impassioned—and more fervent—when they become more personal. The passion is not diffuse but focused if the subjects are his family, his work, or his deepest convictions. He writes of his grandparents and his parents with deep filial love, and it is never forced. His description of his grandfather scything a field is but one example. Sorting beans on a table-top with his grandmother (Nonna) is another (and perhaps the best), but it has the same authenticity as his final days with his father helping him in his bedroom while he waits for him to say something or anything. His poetic feelings are presented as he knows them—without disguise, as in his distaste for some of the work of Robert Lowell or his mature love for the songs of Billie Holiday. Unlike many contemporary poets, he is not absorbed with self, nor does he reduce his poems to mere wordplay. His poems are presentations of felt thoughts, and that is why they are memorable.
 -Samuel Hazo

Samuel Hazo is the founder and head of the International Poetry Forum, Poet Laureate of Pennsylvania, and Professor Emeritus of English at Duquesne University.

For Elsie

Contents

Foreward 3
The Lighthouse 8
Descending and Ascending 9
The Miner 10
Billie 12
Spring Lamb 14
Breaking Beans 16
Garbage Truck at the Crack of Dawn 18
The Osprey 19
Her Body 20
Jazz Smoking 21
Night Electrified 22
Notre Dame 23
In the Field 24
Sunday in Pietrabbondante 26
Closed Wounds 28
Winter 30
Cypress Hill 32
Sundays with Nonna 34
Cal 36
Lunch with Walter 38
After Hours 40
I Have Nightmares 42
Grandfather 44
Wrapped in Cellophane for You 46
Cigarette Bob 47
See Me, Father 48
The Lamp and the Post 49
Sample Homestead 50
Acknowledgements 59

The Lighthouse

We talked last night
a collision of two minds,
one flooded in hope
the other, drowning in despair.
An unread book
silently turning pages,
bending corners in all
the inappropriate places.

You were as phlegmatic as your smoker's cough.
Your head was lowered from too much drink
as if you prepared for an execution.
Words hovered around you
and bounced off walls, those hollow walls,
absorbing all the empty conversations
and thousands of repetitions of apologies
that no one really cared to listen to.
It was the beginning of an end
as you quietly shut the door on our life.

We say "I love you" to each other
as if we're throwing a life
preserver to a drowned man.
Words that bonded us together
are now chards of syllables,
flicked by a melted candle,
a faded beam from a lighthouse that
we can't view from our vantage
point in the dark cold sea.

Patrick Vitullo

Descending and Ascending

An old lady fell to the floor.
Lying there with her head
atop the floorboards,
she heard the music of termites
chewing through the hoist beams.
She could smell the Pine Sol wood.
She imagined that the oily, pine-minty
fragrance protected her from failing
health so she was not afraid.

She dreamt of her youth
when in her native Mayaguez,
she sang on the local radio station
the pulchritudinous ballads of Laura,
Velasquez, and Matamoros.
In those amber, sun-drenched days,
when her lipstick glowed like glossy vermilion,
and her eyes carried the listener of those
Spanish ballads to another time,
she was the queen of the Victrola.

But now, she could barely
crawl to a vacant chair
and hoist herself up.
She cupped her hands
in solemn benediction,
remembering the Spanish love songs
she sang as only she could sing,
content in her new, horizontal world.

The Lighthouse

The Miner

On a liberty boat
the S.S. Dante Alighieri,
a boy from southern Italy
immigrated to America.

By fifteen, in the depths of
a bituminous wall
lighted by a single
kerosene lamp,
he used his pickaxe
to dig for his family
during a time when
miners were considered
lower than the black coal
dust they picked through.

One day, burned
over ninety percent of
his body but cottoned
and salved to life,
he welcomed death
to escape the pain.
Had he ever been
able to hope for
anything beyond
surviving, saving,
and dying?

Patrick Vitullo

The "colored man"
as he came to be called
healed and lived
another 24 years.
Instead of descending into
the hell of western
Pennsylvania coal mines,
he continued to dig every day
in his sunless garden.
The digging never stopped.

Billie

Baltimore and Philadelphia
streets were not a safe haven,
and the blues started
bluein' in you at age ten
when your mother momentarily
quieted your voice
by prostituting you.
And then,
there were also belligerent men
willing to steal, deal, sell,
and drug you at every turn.
Why didn't they just
share in the glory of the
instrument that was your voice?

A force of vocal splendor,
your one-octave voice
was a mix of gravel and glory
and its sound was much
older than your lifetime would ever be.
Louie knew your voice's unbounded capacity.
So did Sinatra who forever thanked
you for the singing lesson.
Modestly, you told him to just bend
the last notes of his songs which
helped to create one of the greatest
male voices of the 20th Century.

Patrick Vitullo

You were obviously
the greatest female voice
to torch and blues it away
whether at Café Society or before
a horde of people at Carnegie Hall.

"Strange Fruit" was unleashed
on the world, a power greater
than just voice and song and was
rightfully forced on closed hearts
in small cafes and concert halls.

Everyone agrees that "Strange Fruit"
was your defining work, but not for me.
I would just like to have one moment in my life
when I can listen to "Lady in Satin" without
crying out for a woman I never met but
loved with the vibration of every note she sang.

Spring Lamb

I was ten years old,
it was spring
and I witnessed violence
like I never witnessed before.
My father and uncle,
men that I loved,
held down a young spring lamb,
its legs bound with heavy twine
on a rusted metal table
fear flamed from its eyes.
It plaintively bahhed
as if some invisible lamb brigade
would save it.
Its face was saying "I'm not your color,"
"I don't speak your language,"
but "help me."
But no one did.
Like me,
they just watched,
from a distance,
too afraid to interrupt the sacrifice
and in one last attempt
to save itself,
overcome with grief and the anxiety
of impending death,
the lamb peed and shat
on my uncle's leg.
He laughed, and shhed it quietly,
in a dialect Italian,
stroking its back.
And then, in one quick stroke,
slit its throat.

Patrick Vitullo

The arterial spray of what remained
of its life colored the driveway's grey gravel
a gossamer red.
Then, the bahhing stopped,
and with one final hind leg twitch
the dead black eyes
stared straight at the torpid sun.

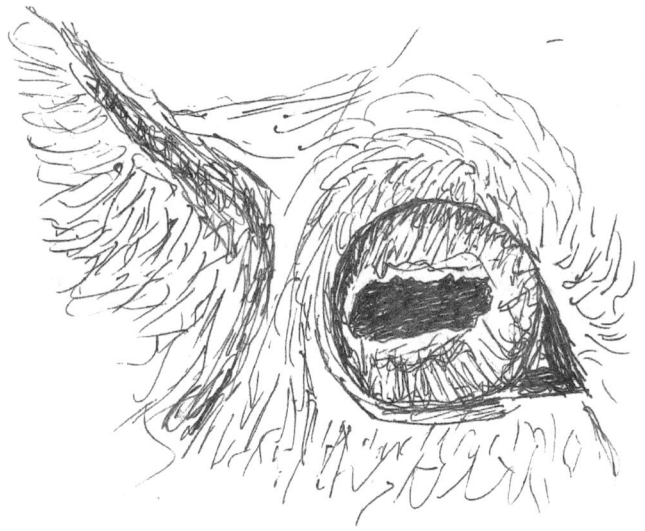

Breaking Beans

Nonna and I sat there breaking beans—long, green, string beans just picked from her summer garden. We filled up cavernous metal pots, pinging with every bean quill that fell to the bottom. I noticed Nonna's silvery hair neatly tied in a bun, which could easily unravel and fall to her bottom.

Then, that grimy guy called "the egg man" arrived, bringing eggs and carrying crates of live chickens. "Here's a good one for you, Mum," he said.

Nonna grabbed the cackling bird by the neck, readied her knife, and before I could scream for her to stop, a river of red poured, which later turned to a golden broth that was pure essence of chicken.

But that was the 1960s, when I summered as a young boy—Now, I walk past the rotted, wooden boxes on Philadelphia's Ninth Street into Pete's House of Chicken for split breasts. If you buy seven pounds, Pete gives you a dozen eggs for free, but the chicken breasts are yellow, not the color of the chickens Nonna bought from the egg man. String beans are a dollar fifty a pound, but too soft and too clean of garden dirt to be the beans we broke together back then. But if I listen closely, I sometimes still hear the lyrical snaps of the bean quills falling against metal pots.

Patrick Vitullo

Figurine

Jeweled, paraffin eyes
melting with ease into
a glow iridescent,
a glistening crescent.
Near I draw, surrendering
touch to imagination.

The two of us pirouette and pivot
like Casanova and his manikinned maiden.
Beneath a laughing moon,
our return to forever
dancing until vertigo overwhelms
our twin hearts, twice-removed,
twice-willed, twice taken into
the one ecstasy of annihilation

Garbage Truck at the Crack of Dawn

6:30 am, a township garbage
truck waddles down the street.
Though my head is covered with pillow,
corroded steel still crescendos
as it moves closer to the windowpane.

The screech of brake pads,
metal gears, and compressors
compact this week's trash and
remind of life's ephemeral motions.
Like a hydra,
the truck hoists its sprocketed head,
tensing up to the a cappella of steel,
compacting corrugated bottles and cans.

As I try to get a few more minutes of sleep,
I question if a life can also be compacted
and thrown away like refuse?
As the thought continues to reverberate,
the shrill noise of the girded truck
travels past the front door and into
an opaque morning's mist.

Patrick Vitullo

The Osprey

With every stroke of oar human effort strives to part water from weed chart the clear sky-reflected path between the cypress tops and move from swamp-still stagnation to undarkened, brisk spring surge.

At the fork in the river the osprey dips its beak in quiet consultation with the wild green. He sees the oncoming machination, but you fail to realize his awareness
vainly attempting to reach the bird and instead circumnavigating a course from river bank to river bank.

Finally, the prodigious oars drop, and you kiss your calloused palms and gaze while the upstream current flows down. Motionless before the implacable fish-hawk, the boat halts, a colossus broken down. The babel of river animals quiets.

You want to strike the oars, freeing yourself from this water bird's world, but you wait as if waiting could make you skim the water, adroit and swift like an osprey.

Iridescence mingles with the brilliance of the sun abounding from his beak as you stare with curious eyes. Then, a sudden splash as he dips his beak! Finally, you can proceed.

Her Body

She experienced
considerable problems
but wasn't a patient.

So, there's only limited
clinical history available:

Her body is well nourished.
Hair is gray/white,
eyes are brown.

There's no palpable, symmetrical,
rounded evidence of medical intervention.
Usual disclosing musculature shows
numerous broken ribs identified.
Present—signs of congestion.
Surface is smooth and
glistening—grossly unremarkable.

Eighty-eight years old with
clinical suspicion of dementia.

One day, she requested
help from her son to get
to the bathroom.
Later, she would be found
slumped over and unresponsive.

Patrick Vitullo

Jazz Smoking

Azure clouds lilt about the room,
hold a token pause, then dissipate
in a cool, blue down-beat
like a waning sax.

A match flicks the stage bright.
A burly man walks, looks, stops
and slows to a chromatic step,
so very even
that it is syncopated.

A woman's hair rassles
like ribbon-cut tobacco
but burns much slower.
A man dottles around
as if he were chipping
a plug from a pipe,
smoothing the crown,
buffing the bowl
and rubbing the wood
to a day-grease shimmer.

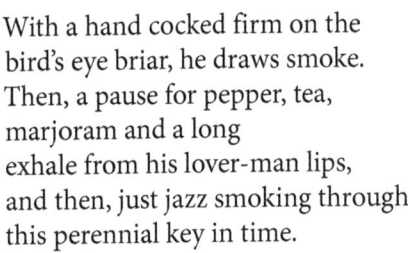

With a hand cocked firm on the
bird's eye briar, he draws smoke.
Then, a pause for pepper, tea,
marjoram and a long
exhale from his lover-man lips,
and then, just jazz smoking through
this perennial key in time.

Night Electrified

A mask of gray crowds the sky.
Nothing can control
the movement of clouds
as if a long, invisible hand
rubbed the back of the sky.

Without warning it detonates,
a crash of sound and
the night is electrified.
Everywhere wind is heard
talking to deciduous and
waving stalks of trees.

It's as black as an unlit highway tunnel
circumnavigating towards such
omnipotence while watching glass
droplets fracture the ground and
smolder at the feet like liquid fire.

Patrick Vitullo

Notre Dame

Was its best face seen from
the Quai de la Tournelle,
Pont de L'Archeveche,
or Square Jean XXIII?
Whether the proboscis of facade
or the gothic grey body worded
and etched from the bookseller's stalls
on the Quai de Montebello,
every look was different.

An arch of neck brought one up
its twin towers and shunned down
the spouting gaff of gargoyles.
Its rose window bloomed before the Seine
while pigeons peripatetic gathered
en masse before a statue of Charlemagne.

A man bedecked in the
beauty of his language
asked for francs, a baguette,
and then, when none were offered,
simply said, bonjour.

Like the countenance of its people,
that lean church beveled
its spire to the sky.
As Emmanuel tolled
solemnly the moment when
Christ died, the Elysian arms of
Our Lady buttressed
the man's tired hands.
And all Paris
foamed in the wake of a bateau-mouche.

In the Field

With a white straw hat and
striations of muscle and calluses,
he looked like a bronze bull
from a distance.

As the sun blazed across the
Pennsylvania summer field,
nothing moved but the old man's hands
arching the scythe in a metronomic
movement back and forth.
It's chrome-like sparkle blinded the rust
on the handles and occasional blood
from calluses that broke open.
Across the high grass,
the rhythm of the old man's
cutting was hypnotic.

His simple labor brought to rest
the monotony of twentieth century automation.
Cars on a nearby highway drifted
to a sheen of silence while the only noise
was the steady, solemn sway of the steel
across the coppled tops of field grass.
Robins paused their flight to stop and listen.

Patrick Vitullo

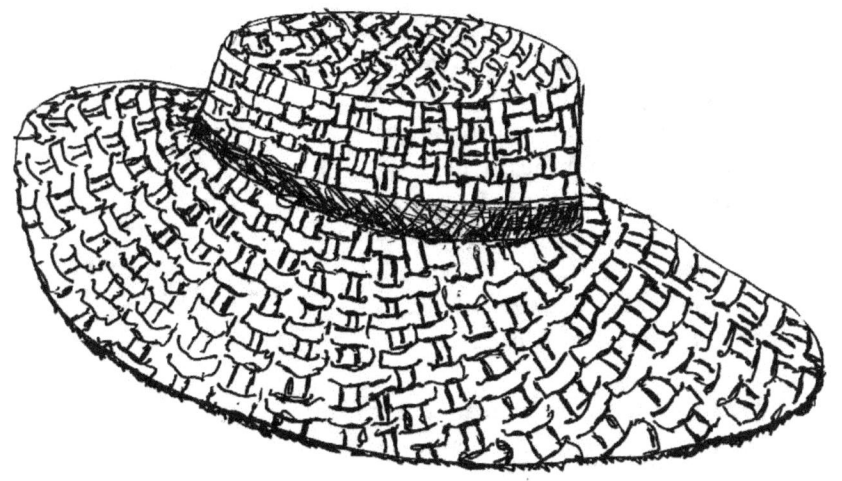

Sunday in Pietrabbondante

The air and sun are
sacrosanct in Pietrabbondante.
A distant son of *il Sanniti*,
inhabitants of the *Sannio*, I'm here
in this Italian mountain village
plotting a course that terminates
at the top of *la Morgia*.

Two generations of navigators at my side
interrupt each other with favorite anecdotes
while villagers below
scream for Marlboro cigarettes
and then fight for the privilege
to cook for the *Americani*.
There we walk,
tripping along the *Via del Piazza*,
past the *famiglia de Gambriaria*
and *la casa de Macedonia*.

We walk past an old woman selling fruit.
"*Vendita per frutta*," she shouts,
crouched over and walking on cobblestone streets.
The sun's rays reflect the church of Santa Maria
and off the woman's carbuncled chin.

Patrick Vitullo

One of the abundant rocks
of Pietrabbondante
falls and finds my forehead.
Blood trickles down my temple,
following a tributary to my heart.
Embracing an iron cross
I find peace at the precipice of *La Morgia*.

Ancient anguish surges in my soul
when I gaze at a statue of Aries
with his shield and sword
warning all who enter to be wary.
Then, I purchase a few *lire* of figs
and sit next to Aries to dine.

Closed Wounds

Wounded man—left for dead
blood streaming from mouth,
eyes swollen and black.
Along his side, police dogs bark loudly
showing fangs and tearing at dirty clothes.

Standing over him,
I tried to give him water,
and hold and comfort him.
He rolled what was left of his eye.
Bloody and tired, he started to cry.

Darkness was everywhere as a
long day moved into evening.
Blood was covered as was the
brutality of American culture,
a closed-head wound
of anonymous meaning
divorced from all
compassion, gasping for but
not receiving the air of sanity,
just lying there
slowly asphyxiating from a
passion play of black versus white.

Patrick Vitullo

Winter

Entranced by the façade of ice
that entraps your vision,
you sit restlessly and attempt
to escape the vertigo of silence
that surrounds you.

Your fingers, numb and lean
reach for a warm place and
instead find three-dimensional
frostbite and vacant scenery.

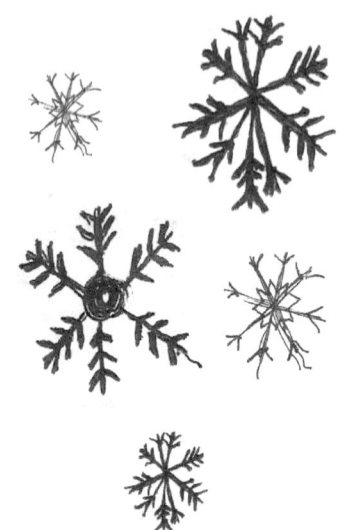

The solitude unnerves
while you communicate
with staccato shudders,
persevering with yourself
and blanketing your desires.

But you're aware that you're
far from alone.
The wind howls hello.
You respond by raising your thermostat.
And the contest continues until you feel
as dried as prunes.

Patrick Vitullo

Peering beyond a sea of ice
nothing but nothing can be more than
white.
It kisses the evening darkness
and warns you that you have a right
to love.

Realizing manufactured warmth
will not heal your injury
you dash to the door,
open it and walk.

It locks behind you and
traps you in wind, night,
and whiteness.

Reckless and withered,
your hollers have no cadence.
You want to cry, but do not.
Instead you stand motionless
and freeze.

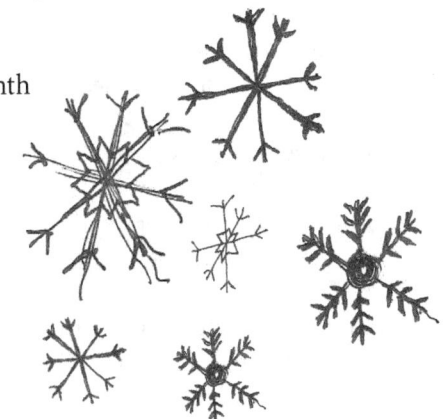

Cypress Hill

There is a wind atop the hill
blowing through her hair
softly uncurling the black mane
with stallion speed.

There is no whistling heard, only
coloring the adumbration of her smile darkly
until the horizonless panorama is linked by
the oscillation of rolling leaves.

Whenever the sun's torpid body lies,
its wounds are momentless to the passage
of time, solemnly slipping through an
hourglass vault to the sea.

Whomever the tears of her touch encumber slowly
a diadem of mounted exaltation is captured by
the benediction of her eyes.

There is wind atop the hill howling
to the upswell of all life's quiet contemplations,
looming like the day's long dagger before the dusk.

Patrick Vitullo

Sundays with Nonna

When I was a child, I lived in a house flanked on both sides with close relatives who showered me with love. Uncle Fred and Aunt Reda were in the house to my left, and my grandparents, Nonno and Nonna were on the right. My grandparents' house was a two-story, red-brick farmhouse built in 1822. When his wife and two sons arrived on a liberty boat from Naples in 1947, Nonno purchased his house and 92 acres of land for about $7,400, using money he'd saved working as a coal miner in a local slope mine called the Wildwood Mine. So, our family members all got to live next door to each other.

Growing up in rural, western Pennsylvania, there was never any boredom. When I played with my neighborhood friends, a game of hide and seek could take up the entire day. I attended a local Catholic grade school and went to church services with my parents on Sundays. As soon as service ended and we returned home, I would run next door to Nonna's house to taste meatballs and sauce because, on Sundays, she'd always prepare the family's luncheon. Of all my childhood experiences, the most special was being Nonna's official pasta and food critic.

Nonna was always in the same dark blue dress with an apron and the same dark black, mid-wedge shoes with support hose. She was a fair-skinned redhead with a mane of long, red hair that could drop to the bottom of her spine but was always tightly pinned up in a bun. She had a strict countenance and her face was weathered from years of hard labor as a farmer in her native, south central Apennine town in the province of Isernia. If Botox had existed in her day, Nonna would have surely used it for her complexion because she was vain.

As she stood by the four-burner gas stove every Sunday, stirring a black-patinaed sauce pot with her signature wooden spoon, there was a comforting sound as the spoon rotated around the metal pot. She pushed the sauce and meat that had been marinating at a very low simmer for hours.

The meat always consisted of chicken, pork, and sometimes lamb but was featured front and center with several tender meatballs made from a mixture of pork, beef, parsley, cheese, and breadcrumbs. Nonna never chopped or minced garlic like so many other Italian-American cooks did. Instead, she thinly sliced the garlic and let the slices float in the oil until brown. Then, she extracted the garlic from the pot before the tomato sauce was added so that there was only a hint of garlic in the sauce. Consequently, her sauce was never overly garlicky.

When it was time to assert the special privilege of being Nonna's food taster, the feeling was always the same – a comfortable waft of gustatory warmth over my mouth from the coalescence of flavors in the meat and tomato. It's a feeling that I will never forget, not just because of the good food but also because of Nonna's love for her family and for me.

The Lighthouse

Cal

For Robert Lowell

Cal, when they told me you considered suicide
after your last walk into the ward,
I thought I would just build a castle
near the ocean, and play poet the hard way
—from my allegorical self.

Don't you remember the voyage you took
into Baudelaire's mind?
Studying life, imitating history.
Notebooks and notebooks
were compiled for Lizzie and Harriet,
far from the land of unlikeness.

No, Cal, maybe you didn't wave the Old Glory
for the union dead or maybe you didn't emulate
Commander Lowell and the Old Flame,
but you began in the 1930s,
day by day
from the Fourth of July in Maine until Christmas.

You failed miserably like every great writer.
Instead of finding the lost fish,
you found a mermaid emerging.

Patrick Vitullo

Lunch with Walter

For Walter Rich

He sat there every summer in Biarritz,
his cane hooked on the back of
his favorite park bench,
overlooking the Atlantic Ocean.

What was he thinking:

the luncheon at the Hotel du Palais,
the remarkable foie gras chaud aux truffes noir
or the Lafite-Rothschild, its superb
crimson rim and aroma of cedar and tar.

Or the camp in Pau,
when he was passing the leftover food
from the dead Jewish captives to the living,
moving quickly with the celerity of a child,
watching and waiting for the moment to escape.

Or when he was driving south
from Philadelphia to Mexico City,
passing through Brownsville, Texas,
with friends, drunk and cavorting about the country,
making up for lost time.

Or the Rue Cherche-Midi,
walking the Rive Gauche to another
dinner at Chez Josephine, in his beloved Paris,
sharing culinary stories with chefs
and sommeliers – his comfortable crowd.

Patrick Vitullo

Or his mother, the only other
relative to leave Germany alive with him
until he lost her too when she went mad from
the stoic repetition of mass family murder,
sixty-four in all, once familiar faces
who never saw freedom after 1933.

Or his friends,
ensconced at his favorite
private dining room table,
bottles of aged Bordeaux aerating,
as they tried to cover up their
jubilation over the cache of
the best wines of the world while he told
the server who brought water to the table,
"No thank you, I've already bathed today."

Or was he thinking about me,
as I sat next to him at the Oyster House,
and he recited story after story like my grandfather.
He cautioned me about my weight,
as we both slipped
our half-lobsters in butter sauce,
and said "living is the best revenge."

The Lighthouse

After Hours

Your fine metal hands
comb the sand to the sea.
Your horizonless eyes
always whisper in the wind.
They're like a looking glass
reflecting its shape in crystal.

You mold meaning
figure feeling
and etch the sound of some long-lined cadence.
A twilight flicked by the heavy hue of the
sun's drowning rays,
a dream meant to be drawn.

Your spouting lips open and close
moist like a fruit's interior.
From our core we learn our
envy for each other.
Stronger than granite and
chiseled in pieces,
it dusts our feet
and crumbles beneath us.

Patrick Vitullo

I Have Nightmares

After telling me that I have
obstructive sleep apnea and wake
100 to 125 times per night
because of lack of oxygen which
causes temporary asphyxiation,
my doctor asked me if I have nightmares.

Do I have nightmares?
I *do* have nightmares:
every time the death toll rises
from Hurricane Maria because
my president did not consider the
Puerto Rican people worthy to be given
sufficient health aid to survive a catastrophe.

and when our president calls the
news media an "enemy of the people" to stoke
hatred and bigotry to assuage his base.

or when American citizens in an American city
drive their automobiles over innocent
protesters, killing or maiming them for
the crippled cause of hateful white nationalism.

and when my government repudiates its
allies but hugs recognized dictators
who torture their people just to appease
his contorted, misinformed base electorate.

or when I watch law enforcement officers
in this "free" country kill the
very citizens they are supposed to aid
simply because of fear over the shade of their skin.

Patrick Vitullo

and when my president
mollifies the National Rifle Association
and sanctions its conduct so that this
merchant of death will continue to
refuse to alter its policies for the
sake of artillery sales, and aid and abet
continuous mass killings while blaming the
deaths on the state of mind of the shooter.

or when I travel to foreign countries and their
citizens laugh in my face because my president
is the paradigm of the "ugly American"
bringing back an antediluvian image of
all Americans as avaricious,
ill-bred, and uneducated.

and when my president says that he will
build a "wall" to keep the vicious brown
gangs out of our country and protect
women from human trafficking
while he enters serial,
extra-marital affairs with younger women,
sealing their lips with non-disclosure agreements,
broadcasting to the media that he can grab
any woman's genitalia he desires.

or when my nephew approaches me and asks me why
the president hates so many people who do not
look like him and why the president shouts all the time.

I have nightmares when I look back
at my nephew without an answer.

Grandfather

Bronze, cigared, and bold,
not quite a hundred years old
a fork in one hand, a knife in the other,
he was not my father, uncle, or brother.

He had a gleam in those swaggered eyes,
a half-filled glass of red,
garden green beans, oil, and garlic
and slice upon slice of homemade bread.

His musty sweat smelled of field
weed, sumac, and fresh cut grass
from the morning's tilling,
raking, and digging of his land.
Self-automated, he pushed
with muscles and bare hands.

With a wicker cap in summer,
a denim blue one for autumn shade,
smoke from a fire-borne stogie would
signal and circle above his head.

He was still digging well past eighty-five
while most others were dead or barely alive.

Patrick Vitullo

John L. Lewis's proud countenance was
buttoned on a grindstone table
from days when the company turrets
would machine-gun workers for leaving
fifteen minutes sooner than they were able.

Three o'clock this first Saturday in October,
I twist and turn a wine press as the
purple grape must oozes over.
Watching my white collar life
rushed through corporate sprockets,
I think of grandfather now
as I affix my signature to this
ancestral docket.

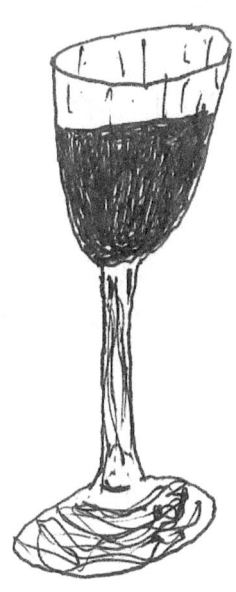

The Lighthouse

Wrapped in Cellophane for You

I'm not your goddess, or your opening hymn of praise.
Instead, I'm shielded from all prejudice and hatred by
the positive translucence of my wrapped body.
My dark eyes will steer your ship
from one port of call to another
until your last wish is to hollow me out from my hull
until I spill over and sink beneath the world's ubiquitous tragedy.

I can break out of this fiberglass cage whenever I wish –
I just don't and freely stand poised for your arms to
unfurl me, curl by curl, until you've unwrapped
and pulled the cellophane off me
until you've realized that's what's really beneath the wrapping.
The decoration
is the
undeniable truth.

Cigarette Bob

Behind the chiaroscuro of a lit Marlboro, there was Bob, smiling and making a proclamation about some obscure wine from his cemetery collection.

You'll be surprised, he pipped about an 82 Paternina Rioja that, under normal circumstances, would make a superb salad dressing. But it was from Bob's collection, and Bob was anything but normal. Driving his manual Saab stocked full of abandoned bottles, he bivouacked through the crawling traffic and searched for a vacant lane. Always an eternal optimist, only Bob would say that his Loire white could outclass any white burgundy on any given day.

Bob was proud of his kitchen skills and proved it when he decided to roast a suckling pig in his home oven without getting his wife involved. *You didn't tell me it would smell so much of pork*, he grunted as Mrs. Bob could be heard screaming the Kosher rules, reminding him never to let a Goy pick dinner. As an honorary Jew, I admired Bob's tenacity to wrestle with a blackened pig and to try to present it as food.

Whether it was a resurrected wine from his graveyard collection or a pithy response to a megaphone friend who hoarded the dinner conversation, Bob's spot at the dinner table, with or without tobacco clouds, made every meal a dining experience.

May Cigarette Bob be with us to his last drag. Then and only then, his dead wines can sit in for him and come alive.

See Me, Father

I look at you now,
the glazed eyes
that silly kid smile and
the forever lost look on your face.
You were a bull of a man
charging up the stairs after work,
your coat draped like a matador's cape.
That stentorian voice
could fade at times to a softer talk.
There were those who couldn't understand your wry wit,
the "how do you feel?" — "with my hands!" style of replies,
the insistence of your points of view,
but not me.
I'm glad we walked together in Italy twice,
once with Uncle Fred tagging along,
telling stories about a lost lover at the Frankfurt train station
who he coveted in his army overcoat and
quietly made love to among busy passerbys.
Or Fausto joking about your old high school antics,
running down main street with the other cadets,
pinching as many young women as you could.
Later, Beatrice gave a teary stare as she held your hands,
and Flora, in la cucina, solemnly stirring the risotto ala forno.

You and I watched the Pietrabbondante house tops from La Morgia
while all of Orte Vecchia's verdant green
sunned itself before us.
Now, you sleep on the toilet until dawn
and your unread face says little.
Still, if I look deep into your eyes,
and talk Italian slowly,
you will see me.

Patrick Vitullo

The Lamp and the Post

The flame was burning orange and yellow
burning on the corner of the wooden post
in the patina crusted lantern,
burning longer than the night's eyes could see
into the maw of morning.
You could see light from far away, from any
dismal corner whether at sea or land.
It brought people together, closer to real reason for life
without the necessity of destruction, of
tearing down the old with new ways
of bringing back the dead from their forgotten ground
and not living the lie again and again.
The flames burn orange and yellow tonight
on the corner of the wooden post
in the patina crusted lantern
waiting to be seen.

Sample Homestead

#1

The old Sample homestead, portentous and proud,
chiseled its firmament against the black-beaten
windless sky.
Addressed by the frozen ground,
two hundred years now, and still,
a picture of lapping rolling meadows,
bringing the dreamscape of our memories
tumbling together as if present.

Echoes of children playing,
a black dog's wagging tail
and serendipity of catalpa beans
hanging limber, swaying slowly from the wind.
Touching the heads of those passing,
looking, not knowing, watching but evading
the transparent twilight of this generation, this figure of God.

There, an old man's bronze skin glistens in sunlight,
his shoulders hunched, dragging a plow
as the whirlwind of smoke chimneys up the cloud-spackled sky.
His face is nonplussed, hushed in muscular strain.
He steps periodically, moves forth, as if
tunneling in open spaces,
nursing the ground's moist upswell with every step.

Felines follow by his side
and dodge willy-nilly at grasshoppers,
still silver maples map the greened lawns while
blades of grass lilt forward as if lulled by a seductive wind.
Propped atop a wooden rake, like a circus canvas on its supports,
an old woman seizes her husband's attention with a litany of expletives

having the incisional skill of a surgeon.
The two conjoin before the backdrop of the old home,
ominous and tranquil,
a hulking giant that assuages the meek and uninspired.

#2
I would smell mother's cookies waft upward from
the kitchen while Grandpa's smiling face poked through
the screen door for a garbage can left unemptied.
His hands full of fresh corn, ripe, rotund tomatoes
and lattice-leafed lettuce that graced the table, fanning out like a
peacock's tail.

When Grandpa disciplined us
he would slap his heavy miner's belt
and dust sprayed from his armchair,
a warning that the second slap would
target a wayward buttock.

We ate the products of the property,
tasted Grandma's goading cadence in every bite.
Grandma was the paradigm of beneficence,
a foreign saint that waked my earth,
her sandblasted skin
all sunned and dry, and all day's nights
would jettison from her working hands.
She was my father's mother, my work, my play,
every day, the umbilical cord to my ancestry.
I can still smell the acidy sweetness of pomodoro,
sticking on the old, wooden bench
where she worked with my aunt and mother,
pressing the tomatoes. I watched the red juice
run free like vermilion, running its bottled course

The Lighthouse

until Sunday when it was seen and then tasted from
a simmering kitchen pot, its scent wafted up into the sky.

The old home
close to Wildwood Road, the
road that led Grandpa, the miner,
to daily aching labor at
the slope mine.
Where did they go,
those heavy coal trucks…
This was only yesteryear, I told myself.
There will be tomorrow.

I was young then, and watched him
shoot coal up its sloped landing to the sun.
I could guarantee that their rumbling tires
approached and would wind me from my walk,
a comfortable fright,
but never so much at ease since their rolling
wheels moved what has remained unmoved.

#3
 Was it the seventh or eighth "Hail Mary"
that reminded me to fear death.
Dreams remained dark as that Thursday morning.
All quiet, I encircled around the hospital's brick walls,
my mind whirling but targeted that single destination:
E-1-L.
Sirens peeled at my closed curtain mind.
Winter, spring, summer, night—all beneath me now,
all fallow and cold.
But I saw the sun in her socketless eyes,
staring at no one.

Patrick Vitullo

I rose that day from chiseled ground,
and cried at night, eating leftover chocolate cookies
for a week while I felt the point of Death's stinging
stiletto darting in and out, every afternoon waking me from
my day-sleep.

Everyday, a fulcrum shot off-balance by mental minutes.
Bivouacking the spherical eclipse of my youth,
waving a hideous hand from the grave.
Grandpa's tears admixed with his cereal when he heard
the bad news.

When we entombed her, I could feel the enormity of her
memory.
It flashed before me like an aerated deck of cards.
What was the meaning?
The sentences of life parsed in gentle phrases before me.
I awakened to those floating phrase-words
in abysmal sea of nonsense
and found meaning where there was none to be found.
I pieced that stillness of those moments before leaving
the phantasmagoric puzzle behind forever
only to return
to revolve,
to re-run again, and again.

#4
Home is where the heart lies.
La casa e dove grace il cuore.
This façade of ice,
a burning frost that melts
from me and singles down into a molten chasm,
a never-ending stream of still, languid experiences
entrapped by the predictable repetition of life.

The Lighthouse

Before the textbook closed
and the dust and mold
blew forth from the past,
my today became yesterday.

My life—story after story of precedent growing atop
a concrete fundament of misunderstanding.
The lesson learned without education.
I accepted it without dialogue, without confrontation.

Today I eat when I'm not hungry
drink when I'm not thirsty.
My body grows in every direction.
Many days, I occupy beds where I don't belong
covered with sheets, tattered and stained
compromising myself for no price.
I walk the straight line to a nether world of neurosis,
and awaken with a hundred kisses from inexact lips.
This is where all knowledge resides,
swirling furiously in a vortex of ignorance.

#5
The Chthonic Woman and Old Man are friends.
They meet at the square, near Mandala Street
every afternoon. Eyeing a half-moon drink
she points her bony finger at his mouth.
His lips touch her fingertip and part to open.
He gestures with his tongue once, twice, and around
the perimeter of her finger. Then, as he swallows
the residue of his love for her, he kisses her
lonesome smile goodbye.

They can never leave each other.
No break in time, only a collage of feeling rotating
like the seasons. From the first sappy spring until
the dead of last winter, they are always recurring,

Patrick Vitullo

sometimes a little warmer, others, a little cooler.
Now, with his hands clutching solidly
the iron rails of the Notre Dame grotto,
the snow strikes the staccato tempo of his lips.
He watches the snow reflect the candle-flames,
a silhouette of un-carried acolytes still.

His mind meanders down the last summer walk with her.
A wooded path that allowed only rivulets of light and
cicada calls. Their simultaneous footsteps
and locked hands were louder than voices.

#6
 The detectable scent—the burnt crisp of decayed leaves
penetrates the cloying residue of sunlight.
The dust of the crawling road has settled,
the old depravity remains chilled from last night's frost.
Somewhere in this autumnal stillness, there is memory.
A memory that spots the hills with crimson
rust-orange and faded yellow.
A memory that reminds me
the feast is never finished.
There, on a single unoccupied tree limb,
hovers a brooding wind.
Something inside it whirls furiously.
A mood maybe or possibly the
rapture of the terminal moment.
This apotheosis of the seasons,
this twist of day to night—as a scattered breeze
in the chill night air—it all remains damp like the
autumn leaves. Tomorrow, we will remember.
There, in the barest patch of ground
stands a sycamore. Its denuded bark
welcomes the solitary wind to an
outsound of birds flocked for the southern warmth.
The sycamore peaked

The Lighthouse

like a wooded needle to the sky
remained motionless in the winged
horizon of these frenzied creatures.

Her face reappeared, wanton and alone.
That tilted smile embraced my body once again.
With its inward maneuver,
my lips unwound like a skein dethreading.
In the rust spackled glare of dusk,
we held each other over and
against time's deceptive glare.

#7
 The grapes, the grapes.
Clumped in rotund bunches of thirty or more, they remained
fast to the vine. Their glistening wetness atop the black-purplish skins
brought tears to the old vintner's eyes. His heart, laden with life's
prosaic chores, passed from this world and ascended into heaven as he
carted the unctuous fruit. No sounds were audible as he heaved the
pulpy crate to
the mouth of the piggaitrice and churned the handle, feeling
the resistance of tiny bundles against the sprockets of steel, as his
leftward hand
guided the sappy ooze of grape toward its penultimate demise.
He sung Italian songs as the crates passed purple hands hastily and
became
a debridement of cracked wood, stained but alone, like an empty
lover's bed.

#8
As the days passed,
the old vintner inspected the lot.
The pulps now incandescent,
now spark-shimmering in the brooding
hull of the barrel.
The alcohol spewed off the wood and dried,

Patrick Vitullo

ink-purple stems hovered
among the balls of seeds.

His hands—stained with zinfandel juice.
His eyes perennially teared.
From his stove-dried lips rose
a hum of il canzone de la campanella
as the staves creaked from the twist of the
spoon-turn of his arms.

On the eighth day, the black-rust of the
bolted press, ominous and old, occupied the
cement floor.
The free juice of the pink-purple grapes spilled
into a half-barrel on the cellar floor.
The moon hung above the cellar window and
cast the only light, the sole guide through the
pitch silence of this eternal evening song.

It was manganza, the hour of pressing the grapes,
the moment when the vintner created the wine.
As he filled the press with the handfuls of leaking
pulps, his eyes were filled with prayer.
He was afflicted by the ageless passion of his wine-
making—his bittersweet bondage with the land.
He torqued the metal arm of the wine press,
positioned the wooden, crusted block for leverage,
and heaved the hull of his body for the turning
into and away from the grapes.
The kind juice perspired over the staves of the press,
then trickled until it burst open into rivulets of
young sweet wine only to be caught by the mouth
of the press, encircling to the spout and
released into the sea-pan of the old vintner's
wanton arms.

Acknowledgements

There are several people that have helped bring this book to fruition, in one way or another, over the last forty plus years. First, I acknowledge the several hours of editing, collaboration and commentary from Ayesha Hamid, my editor and editor-in-chief of The City Key. Her contributions provided much needed focus. Special thanks to Sam Hazo for such a generous Foreward, and for introducing me to the spoken art of poetry from the Duquesne years and many recitals at the International Poetry Forum. Special thanks to Melissa Broder for providing guidance and inspiration on publishers, and Peter Nalle and Rochelle Davis for reviewing, editing and commenting on this book. Thanks also to The Antigonish Review for its publication of "Spring Lamb" and the City Key for publication of "Notre Dame." Thanks to Colleen Cummings for her superb editing, illustrations, and cover work. A special thanks to my wife, Madeline, for her patience and commentary, and Sam, my bull terrier, who taught me perseverance and provided many a contemplative moment during our walks. To Tony Caridi for being a catalyst for my literary career back in "The Room, " circa early 70s, with copious philosophical and literary conversation. To those who are no longer in this world but very much a part of this book including my parents, Anthony and Elsie Vitullo, my paternal grandparents, Pasquale and Margherita Vitullo, my mother-in-law, Casta Hadee Echevarria (I can still see you singing the Spanish boleros in my kitchen), my late wine friends, Walter Rich and Bob Broder (hopefully God is serving some First Growths to you somewhere), and for the many friends who have asked me about this book and encouraged me to write over the years. Finally, this book is not possible without Krish Singh, publisher and owner of Auctus Publishers, who believed in me and provided a home for this work, and hopefully others to come.
   –Patrick Vitullo

www.ingramcontent.com/pod-product-compliance
Lightning Source LLC
Chambersburg PA
CBHW072107110526
44590CB00018B/3353